Songs of Desire

written by:
Desiree Lamphier

*One thing I have desired of the Lord,
THAT will I seek:*

*That I may dwell in the house of the Lord
ALL the days of my life,*

*To behold the beauty of the Lord,
And to inquire in His temple.*

For in the time of trouble He shall hide me in His pavilion;

*In the SECRET PLACE of His tabernacle
He shall HIDE me;*

He shall set me high upon a rock.

And now my head shall be lifted up above my enemies all around me;

*Therefore I will offer sacrifices of joy in His tabernacle;
I will sing, yes, I will sing praises to the Lord.*

*Hear, O Lord, when I cry with my voice!
Have mercy also upon me, and answer me.*

**When You said, "Seek My face,"
My heart said to You, "Your face,
Lord, I will seek."** *Psalms 27:4-8*

Dedications:

Jesus~ I would like to take this moment to say... that without you I am nothing but because of you... I truly can do all things; everyday you are my inspiration; everyday we are linked together in a Secret World. I cherish our times together and even still; everyday, everything is fresh and new, so in love with you Jesus!

Thank you to my most beloved Husband Doug~ I loved you in High School and I love you now... forever and always you have filled my heart. Every day you are a gift to me and I love spending time with you!

My beautiful babies~ Savannah and Holly; you make me so proud... Thank you for your encouragement and support as I travel the World telling everyone to love Jesus more and more… (Savannah, Holly Lamphier)

Momma~ I love you, your so special, so sweet... my best friend forever! Thank you for giving me the dream that I can do or be anything… (Sally Cleveland)

Daddy~ Thank you for always being honest and a man of integrity! Thank you for always taking care of me! (Don Cleveland)

What Pastors are Saying:

"I've known Desiree, her husband Doug and their two beautiful girls for 20 years now. I first met Desiree when a friend recommended she come minister at our church. Desiree really KNOWS Jesus. She continues to cultivate a deep intimacy with Him. The result? Real signs, wonders and miracles. She prayed for me after I had been diagnosed with Crones Disease and the Lord miraculously healed me. We have her minister every year at our church. There is a powerful prophetic anointing on her life and she has been raised up as an end-time prophetic evangelist to the world. I have drawn closer to my Lord and Savior as a result of her ministry and I believe you will, too.

Pastor David Alderman

Plainwell Assembly of God
Plainwell, Michigan

"When I think of how PAPA allowed Desiree and my life to come together all I can say is thanks PAPA. The first time I saw Desiree in Thomasville, NC all that I could see was the love of Jesus. Desiree is a atmosphere changer, she brings love to the lowest person and fulfillment to the person that is not sure about a situation. That is the LOVE of PAPA, JESUS, HOLY SPIRIT! Her desire to have intimacy with PAPA, JESUS, HOLY SPIRIT it is the

deepest I have ever experienced. Wanting more and going after more of PAPA, JESUS, HOLY SPIRIT that is Desiree.
I count it a honor to call her my friend and to be apart of her life and apart of what PAPA is doing in her life for others. Desiree is a world changer. Thanks Desiree!!!"

Your friend,
Pastor Linda Suggs

Thomasville Christian Fellowship
Thomasville, North Carolina

"Desiree consistently ministers from a place of intimacy with the Lord and because of this God's glory and love flow freely from her. The Lord manifests his presence in unusual and glorious ways through her ministry so that people have a true and personal encounter with the Living God. Desiree also sets an example for believers in integrity and as a person of prayer. I highly recommend her ministry to anyone hungry for more of God."

In Him,
Pastor Shawna Deihl
Florida

"Desiree is a true woman of God that has brought Gods presence every time she has come to Thomasville, North Carolina.
The time she spends in prayer shows as she changes lives around her. As a witness to God speaking through her with prophetic words and encouragement. I have learned to listen, and have seen the move of God in her services. I can Testify to the miracles and healings. When Desiree speaks you will be encouraged and inspired by the love she has for God as she compels others to that love.
I am convinced that as you read this book you will become more passionate than ever for things of God."

Pastor, Ed Shortt

Whirlwind Ministries
Thomasville, NC

"Desiree is young woman whose heart is set on one thing alone; the presence of
God. From her hours spent in prayer and worship flow and amazing ministry that brings miracles of healing to peoples bodies, prophetic words that encourage and build up, and a renewed zeal to seek the face of God. Spending so much time in his presence has allowed Desiree to get a view of the heart of God. She has proclaimed, "I will love what you love and hate what you hate!" and as a result

has come to love the lost and the dying of the world. She lives to see Jesus get his full reward for the suffering that he did on the cross. As you read this book I believe that you will be taken into many encounters with God. You will get a new glimpse of his face and a new reality of his love for you."

Blessings,
Pastor Kim Tanner

Athens Christian center
Athens, MI

Introduction

Yes, it's certainly true, that one can be so in love with God because He is so amazing! Not a romantic kind of love of that between a husband and a wife but a love that goes to a place deeper beyond that... a deep calls unto deep.. You know the place, it's a place deep inside your heart, a place where the real you lives. It's a place where there are longings deep within your own bowels. In that place we try and find ways to fill those longings with things of the world like sex, drugs, alcohol, television, games, internet, etc. But it always leaves us empty and wanting, needing more. But when we fill that deep place within ourselves with <u>HIMSELF</u>... there is a joy, a completeness; yet a sweet longing for more. He becomes our passion and reason for living every day!

A Three Month Encounter

Have you ever wondered or supposed what it would be like to actually be with Him dear reader? Have you thought or even daydreamed what it would be like to be with Him face to face in His presence like you are with a friend for lunch. I have had this happen and must say it is the most heart wrenching thing I have ever experienced thus far. Simply for the fact that being with Him and then leaving Him.... is pure agony... pure torture, a hurt so deep for Him. And it's not to "sense" Him or to be in His presence but for the literal person of Jesus.

While growing up I have always had a hunger inside for God. As an adult many countless times I would be at the alter weeping because of hunger I had for Jesus. Sometimes I would be at the alter for 2-3 hours weeping. One time I was at a conference where the guest minister encouraged people to stay at the alter for as long as they wanted to seek the Lord. I was there crying out to God, so hungry, pleading with Him to come and visit me... when I felt a tap on the shoulder, it was the custodian asking me to leave cause they wanted to clean the building for the next service! Saddened almost embarrassed and hungry, I got up, left quietly to my car where I sat and continued to seek and cry out to God till the next service.

Let me explain the kind of hunger that consumes me...

*So hungry that I can be praying at night and get sleepy... so I'll go outside in the middle of winter with pajamas on and jump up and down in the snow... telling my flesh "NO, we were going to stay awake and pray."

*So hungry that I will take anointing oil and pour it over my head praying God would visit me and use me.

*So hungry I physically force myself (alone) to stay up all night to pray to God.

*So hungry I will sit in my chair and weep at the end of Church Services. Why? Because the service is over. I would pray desperately that they would last longer.

*Most of the time I leave a Conference or a Service, I feel wounded and will weep because I'm so hungry.

*Sometimes while attending a conference I will miss a service because of seeking God in my hotel room and unable to move because of being so hungry and encountering Him..

*I cancel lunch engagements with friends because of wanting/needing to be alone with Him.

*My pastors (at the time) thought their was something wrong with me because it was not natural to be so hungry, they would say "The Bible says that you hunger and thirst after righteousness you shall be filled so maybe something else is going on" But what the Lord revealed to me a few years later was that you hunger and thirst EVERYDAY AND EVERYDAY He fills you! Or I would hear this continuously "Now Desiree to be too Heavenly/Spiritually minded will do you no earthly good." I literally thought for years... that this was a verse in the Bible! It completely shocked me (years later) that it wasn't!

*I would find myself on my knees in the middle of the night desiring and pleading with for God to use me and to visit me with His deep rich presence.

*I go through seasons and cry myself to sleep at night in bed because of being so hungry for Him and to be used by Him.

*So hungry, I did a meeting in a old store front, over an hour away from home; for three nights and no one showed up... I preached any ways and recorded it.

*I did a meeting at a hotel and God did such mighty things, everyone was on the floor weeping under His amazing presence and many were healed... Then days later I was still weeping over what the Lord had done and could not eat. And became desperate for more of Him and to be used by Him and fell in love with His goodness.

*I will fix dinner sometimes and say to my family enjoy... leave and go pray skipping the evening meal.

*So hungry I cry myself to sleep because of needing Him...

*So hungry that I spend any where from 4-6 hours a day praying.

*So hungry that I will spend all night just worshipping Him.

*So hungry that I will miss meetings/services because of my need to be alone with Him.

*Will cry myself to sleep because of the simple fact that "He is good."

*Will wake up in middle of the night and room will be filled with the presence of God.

*Will weep over the word; (Pslams 119) Will laugh over the word. Get intoxicated with the word.

*Will have joy of the Lord in private time and no one is around.

*Weep over people.

*Full of the peace of God and have great Revelation on living in the fullness of God yet being hungry.
.
*So hungry that I was weeping where He met me on a bridge in Redding California and sent two prophet's one from Bethel staff who prophesied my whole life, Ministry and calling; even included the way I pray and deepest desires were exposed.

*So hungry today; Revelations of intimacy pours into me like no other subject-intimacy with Him is my life; Can't live with out praying or being alone with Him... if their is no "me and Jesus time" their is no Ministry time, no Meeting to be conducting, no one to pray for, no life. He comes first before everyone and anything.

*So hungry that I literally feel His Godly jealousy that He feels. He wants us and doesn't want to share us…

*Hungry that it's only in Him where I can be satisfied and filled.

*Wearing Sunglasses is one of my favorite things... it's a way of hiding in public so you can be in the Secret Place in the midst of a lot of people.

*So hungry that I literally will seek the face of Jesus and will see His face with my eyes open; on a wall or in the surroundings.

So keeping all this in mind... I had an encounter with the Holy Spirit on my birthday February 29, 2008.

On this birthday I asked the Lord for something special from Him. "Anything you want to give me Lord". That night the Lord visited me in such a way I will never forget and it lasted for three months. It was through a worshipful sound of a violin that physically entered my heart during worship. As I listened I heard the Holy Spirit almost audibly say "listen to this" and as I listened to the violin, I literally felt it go deep, deep, inside; into a place so deep that I didn't even know existed inside my heart. And what I heard audibly in that sound was the hunger in my heart being played audibly. Hunger over the last 12 years, secrets in my heart were being played! And it was a sound I was looking for through music, was searching for it...The Lord was playing the hunger in my heart through the music. It was the most amazing sound. As I listened I was frozen and didn't want to move, I wept quietly cause I didn't want to miss any part of that sound. I felt the sound go inside me and this sound messed me up and broke me for the hungriest I had ever been in my life. (Remember the above list) It felt as though the Lord took a nob and turned all the hunger I was already carrying (see above) and turned the hunger ten times hotter. And for three months I was so hungry not for His presence but for the person Jesus. Hungry for Him to come and manifest Himself to me.

During these three months the Lord gave me tastes of what it was like to actually be with Him, the person Jesus. And while it would seem to be wonderful, it was the most awful, most despondent, most heart wrenching hunger I ever experienced. During this time I was not hungry for the presence of God but was hungry for Jesus Himself. The presence of God was not going to fill me like it had in past times. But it was Jesus Himself that I HAD to have. I wept as if I lost someone so dearly... day and night.

Words cannot express the agony I felt. We have heard people say that when someone they love goes to be with Jesus and how they wouldn't want to come back to us on earth. I can honestly say I know what that is like... because to leave His presence (actual person) is the most heart wrenching thing a person could ever go through. It felt like the whole world and every bit of pleasure and enjoyment was completely gone. I couldn't function with day to day activities and found myself lost and staring into space longing to be with Him more and more. I remember I was at a basketball game for my little girl, weeping because of the simple fact that I was wanting Jesus. I told my husband I am so broken for Him. And, I remember this so clearly, I was attending some Revival meetings in a corn field in Iowa. They were outside meetings and I wondered off one night to be alone out in the field in the dark. I NEVER in my life felt so alone, so despondent, so desperate for the person Jesus to come. And in the weeds and dirt I wept and wept, a deep hunger and brokenness I would never want to repeat or impart to anyone. It was almost to the point of where I couldn't bear it any more. I would have to remind myself that "blessed are those that hunger and thirst after righteousness are blessed". So "despondent" this is the actual word the Lord gave me as I was weeping out in the field that night. The definition of despondent is- in low spirits from loss of hope or courage. So hungry for Jesus that they are beyond words and my Spirit man groaned so deep to be with Him. Even talking about it with you now; stirs up an ache inside me (and you right?) to be with Him.

We are a people so in love with Jesus... Could it be this type of hunger is now sweeping across the lands... a hunger not for His presence but for Jesus Himself? Could this be the hunger that will bring Jesus back to rescue us from this World we now live in? A hunger for Him Himself.

Oh my friends this is so deep; it wounds my insides, to be with Him is indescribable and to come away from actually being with Him is that feeling of despondent- low in spirits from loss of hope and courage, because He is our hope, He is our courage, He is our everything. Please hear my words to you this day reader... He is our everything!! For three months, this season lasted and by the end my husband looked at me and asked if I was going to be okay... at the time I wasn't sure. But a few weeks later this type of hunger lifted and a joy filled my heart like never before! I had the joy of the Lord constantly... and was now laughing for hours though out the day. And sounds that I hear now were so different then before. I can listen to someone play an instrument or someone minister the word and know if they have spent time alone with the Lord that week. I hear sounds in the Heaven-lies and show/help worship teams and bands all over the World how to play with a different sound... I know what the heart beat of God sounds like. I know songs that can be totally secular but hear the anointing in them. Recently, the Lord allowed me to hear what it's like when you and I give an offering. It sounds like a magical tinker bell sound! Amazing! Also, I have had times where my ipod was off yet through the head phones I heard music... a whole symphony that I have yet to find here in this World.

He's a lover and he will take no prisoners or wont allow you to make Him come in second, He is jealous for you; longing to be with you in that place of intimacy. For in that place of intimacy no one can hurt you or touch you. You become hidden so the enemy can't find you and doesn't even know you exists when you abide in that place.

Never mind what others say or what others do, focus on the one who created you. He Himself loves you and wants nothing more but to be loved by you first and for most in your life.

It's the deep that calleth unto deep. It's the longing of the other side of heaven that is rooted inside every believer.. the problem is when we don't listen or get to preoccupied with our mind, we get so we can't respond to the cries that He is wooing and drawing you. We become numb or try to fill that deep space with something else so that in doing so we break God's heart.

It's not of works lest any man should boast. But its that quality time that He desires with you and that is where your help comes from.

Allow yourself to let go of natural thinking while reading this book. Free yourself of everything but loving Him. Let this book be about you and your God. Our prayer is that you will love God through the words written. That they are your expressions to Him and if you find that you begin to read a portion then drift off into some deep prayer with Him then so be it! Let this reading be something to ignite you to a passionate pursuit of God Himself. Take your time as you read through these intimate expressions, let them become yours! I give them to you... use them to escalate you into deep intimacies with the Father. Let these words take you deep with Him that you never even dreamed possible. Soar new heights with the King of Kings! Learn a new love language to Him and feel the presence of God come all around you as you love Him with your words.

✧✧✧

And so now I present to you the songs that flow deep within, their is no thought, but a river flowing from the inner most being to the throne room of God. There are blank pages for you to journal and to allow the heart of God to speak to you as you read and pray.

✧✧✧

SONGS OF DESIRE

Deep expression from within long to be taken upward to a higher place in Him. A place where you don't know who or what you are but divinely supernaturally intertwined and truly become one with Him.

✧✧✧

Be certain, there is no mistake. God you are faithful beyond words could ever say. Though the dreams and disappointments have felt delayed, your timing is so right on and can not be denied. So grateful my heart is to thee. Loving your faithfulness and showing me things so bright. Love these times with you nothing can compare. Bring on these plans you have for me and together we will combat the enemy.

✧✧✧

I love your love, Jesus your are so beautiful to me, Your lips are so soft and feel like silk. Your skin is so pure from the Holiness that lies within you. One look of your eyes melts and even steals my heart and it sets people free. Yes, even: Our, eyes set people free because it is you who looks through them and heals with one touch, one look of your love.

✧✧✧

Your demonstration is more then I can understand. Your ways are too deep for me at times to gain the understanding needed. Release oh Lord your divine thrust forward of revelation knowledge. So many things you have put inside; desires that are more than passionate. Come Holy Spirit and breath these fresh possibilities but also give me understanding to move forward in them. I so long to do the works of your love and live my life as a vessel used by the master. I give myself wholly to you my God.

✧✧✧

There is a greater understanding that I must walk in. I must realize what is at my very disposal just below the surface of who I am. Take care-look inward and manifest His goodness outward. Miracles, signs, and wonders are so necessary to live in everyday. People need to see the glory signs oh Lord. Boldness, oh Lord, I need the miraculous power ever displaying in me and through me, for I am your disciple.

✧✧✧

No, I am not lost though sometimes I feel forgotten. Forgotten in the shuffle wondering what it is and why it is this way. But then suddenly God moves and shows His shining face so others can see what is really going on inside this Holy place.

◇◇◇

Sitting and sitting. When will this be over. Longing and waiting for my time to arrive. Time for to arise and shine. Keeping remembrance of all your promises: Oh Lord and making them fresh and anew everyday. But still waiting and longing for the time to come. Give me the platform, give me the stage, I want to step into that place. Don't want to be the spectator, Lord, here am I send me!

◇◇◇

Sleepless nights and peak early mornings we embrace our love together far more then words could ever express. You are my lover and together we make one. Kiss me, hold me and love me all night, embracing your Kingdom, touching your hair, loving your smile, hearing your truth. Nothing can be greater then this rich time with you. Keep me close, keep me the apple of your eye. You are so much greater: nothing can compare. Turn on the light, the light of your revelation so I can behold your beauty and see your face all through the night.

✧✧✧

Carry me away, is all I can pray; Grab hold tight and do not let go. You are the baker and I am the dough... have your way with me I pray.

✧✧✧

Love me, hold me and embrace me Jesus , again. My very depth and heart cry out for the refreshing of all that you are. Draw me close and embrace me; let your hands touch my face for I am yours. I touch your face and kiss you because your so lovely and so sweet. Who can know a man who is so tender in your ways, their is no-one even close to who you are and all that you become to me each day.

✧✧✧

This time is so uneasy. The dream within grasp. I can almost touch it and feel it. But I want to take it now for it is mine. Dream come here!! My mind and body in turmoil wanting to embrace and partake the dream together with you by my side. I can taste the victory on my lips. My heart has been beating for this moment in time.

✧✧✧

Every day I fall in love with you all over again. You are so good and so holy, I can't get enough. Your unfailing love never stops. You never forget, always on time, and you know my name. Allow me to kiss you again once more, to worship you with all that is within me and more. Come to me my love and let us be together all day in the secret place, in the cleft of the rock. In still waters I engage your beauty and get acquainted with you in the Kings Chamber. You embrace me and I embrace you and we don't let go of each other for hours. Each kiss is propelled to another as your words come to me inside my flesh and my love pours over you as you pour over me. Like Enoch, For I was not for God took me.

✧✧✧

Experiences in God are not to be compared. For each one is like a gift from Him; no one would exchange for the World. Believe me when I say His love is better then wine.

✧✧✧

✧✧✧

✧✧✧

You are altogether lovely. Just when I think I cannot love you any more, my heart swells and my love grows yet again. You are the treasure I have found. You are my song I sing. My love for you can not be compared because your sweetness; your goodness is beyond what can be described. My heart, my life, belong to you in a holy way. Everything I do, everything I say reflects who you are to me. Today I am going to preach your Gospel Lord. And if I have to; I will use words…

✧✧✧

Okay, let's see. Look at it this way, one day closer… to discovering the greater within. One day closer to reach the fullness of all that you have for me. One day less, means one day, closer still; to the dreams; to the goals I have. The ones Jesus put inside, the gifts and the callings. One day closer the dream is right before you- grab on to it. I can barely reach… but I keep reaching. I will get it cause I'am a day closer then I was yesterday!

✧✧✧

Embracing Him beyond what words can articulate. He is so real and so wonderful how can anyone not embrace Him. Taking hold of all of Him is what we desire yes even want to do. His words, His embrace, His Holy Spirit, His oneness… Living each moment with Him in us and upon us…

He is our so long hoped for, He is the one we desire every moment of every day; it's Him whispering sweet nothings and making us feel so alive in Him. He is the air we breathe; meaning without Him we cannot breathe.

✧✧✧

Jesus I love you, Jesus I need you!

✧✧✧

I breathe desperately and heavily, Jesus I need you, let me see you face. Carry me away in the reality of who you are while I am here in this place awaiting for the divine appointment to be ever in your arms.

✧✧✧

Take me and breathe upon me at last so we can run together and love each other freely. I hear you calling my name every day to come closer. And without reservation every day I come. I come to you because YOU are the apple of MY eye Jesus. You have a place with me where you can lay your head down anytime. I am awake unto you and Jesus I know YOU by name... I love you back Sweetie…

✧✧✧

Allow me to take you into my arms and allow me to hold you till the day is done. And when the evening is come we will embrace all the more and add beautiful whispers of how much we love and mean to each other. For we are two lovers beckoning one another and we just can't stay apart. Not romantic but a pure love we love deeply.. Your in my thoughts constantly. I think about you all the time. You are my precious Jesus and there is no one in this World like you. You make me happy. It's a state of being I am in all the time because your so magnificent and full of splendor my eyes and my heart are constantly filled with wonder at just a glance... you steal my heart away. Forever you are my beloved Jesus. You are the solid rock and every where else I stand is sinking sand.

I am captivated by your love. Your eyes have locked me into a place of intimacy and I cannot get away; don't want to get away. Your eyes lure me into deep quiet places where my mind is taken over by thoughts of only you. A place where the mind dies and the renewed mind takes over. A place where two hours with you is really five hours in reality... because you swept me away again. Phone rings, dog barks, people beckoning for my attention yet the only thing I hear is a knock on the door of my heart and it's you! I have opened myself to you for yet another encounter another loving moment with you.

✧✧✧

✧✧✧

✧✧✧

Every day is like Christmas

Everyday is like Christmas because you are before my eyes. Each day is a gift because your in it. How I love you my Precious One. You created me, isn't that neat? You made me.... in the image of yourself. This excites me Papa, that you loved me enough to have me look like you, to act like you, and to be with you is a glorious gift!

✧✧✧

Alone. Oh Jesus, sometimes I wish I wasn't alone so much. Please understand my heart, I love being with you again today; just the two of us. But I am alone so much, I have no "close" friends but you. You are my prize possession but when I am alone with no one around it makes me hungrier to be with you in the flesh. When loneliness comes my heart longs for you so much more. But please understand it's not for your presence though your presence is priceless. I hunger for YOU in the flesh, I long for to be face to face, skin to skin, touching you and holding you next to me in the flesh. Even so come Lord Jesus quickly and save us from this lonely World.

✧✧✧

Your presence is so great. I cannot believe how real you are! Your tangible presence is amazing... Your so addictive! Your so alive. Makes me want to scream "Here, over here Jesus is the true God!. Come and feel Him He is so near." Because it's true. If only people could feel you more. Yes, even your people could feel you more, how awesome would that be.

✧✧✧

I am thinking about you this very moment. Your tenderness draws me in and I will not give up, for my eyes will stay on the prize.

✧✧✧

Here you are again... Whooing me, my heart aches and my eyes are wet because of my love for you and all that you are doing. I love you so deeply. So grateful for all that you are doing... you mean so much to me. Because it has taken so long; I am so careful and so grateful for every little thing you do. I appreciate when the phone rings because I remember when it didn't; I appreciate the emails I receive because I remember when I had none; I appreciate having meetings because I remember weeping over being home wishing I was there. Now I weep with gratefulness because the phone does ring, emails I now receive and meetings I have. No one is more grateful then I. Perhaps though I imagine papa there are some…

✧✧✧

Deep interludes go through my being as I entertain your desire towards me. You amaze me to yet another level again today. Desiring to be taken over by you again is all I want.

✧✧✧

What happens when I get into that place of pure ecstasy with you alone. It is so profound; so amazing… Your love is better then sweet things to my tongue.

✧✧✧

What is this, that come out of no-where and moves my heart, my depth inside towards you… It must be you Holy Spirit. Your whooing me to Jesus again. ("Dear Reader of these words, can you feel that? Can you feel that whooing inside you, If not that is okay…some don't feel anything and they find themselves with a desire to pray and spend time with Him… and that is another way He whoos us")… So in love with Jesus!

✧✧✧

No excuses! I have none to give, because my all in all belongs to you and is yours. There is no hesitation, there is no level of being defeated lying within. My hope alone rest in and upon you. You are an everlasting Papa who never lets me down. Being in love with you my hope and my all in all, I stand. Guarding my heart so my love continues to grow for you. But wait! How can that be; my love for you is so much I feel I could explode. Yet guarding is what you say to do... I guard my heart so I can always feel you as close as I do now and guarding my heart so I can hear you speaking to me!

✧✧✧

How does one explain your presence? It's like ecstasy. A miraculous something; someone takes up residence on your skin and you feel him all over you. It is a feeling that is so good... you got to have more! Tingly, heat, coolness, and some ways I can't even explain. No, No... I am not talking about sensing God, but feeling Him touching me! For it is but a glimpse of what Heaven shall be like!

✧✧✧

Every bit of my life belongs to you Jesus. Every single part of all that I am belongs to you, I am not my own I am bought with a price of His blood. Nothing I have belongs to me, nothing good, nothing wonderful, belongs to me. It all belongs to you. My life is hidden in you my beloved.

✧✧✧

Completely in love. Where am I? Can this love be true, can your faithfulness be right? Are you truly that faithful? I am longing for you, now... I feel you my friend, I feel my heart being pulled to a closeness that is not of this realm. My heart is so yearning, what can help my insides release these longings... I know, you only.... come quickly…

✧✧✧

Just a glimpse of your glory and it touches my heart; so sweet, so amazing, truly you are no respecter of persons. I have seen you touch entire assemblies and it blesses me, so that all I want is more…

✧✧✧

The way you dote over me my Lord and my King, you leave me speechless and your mercy, tenderness, and sweetness is beyond anyone or anything this World has to offer...

✧✧✧

✧✧✧

My heart yearns for you to move. My heart yearns to see your smile, my heart longs and needs desperately an encounter of true revival of love...
Grateful... thank you my Lord... so grateful to you. You are amazing beyond words, you truly are the most humble person I know, you are someone I look up to and my aim is to be like you... help me Holy Spirit to be like Jesus…

◇◇◇

My greatest desire is only you; I pay no thought to anything else. All I want is you.

◇◇◇

Can you imagine; no I cannot. To be with you in Heaven; selah. To be WITH you my love is my greatest passion. Take a knife- open the bones that enclose my chest, take out my heart; dissect it and you will only find it broken and full of love for you.

◇◇◇

You are the air I breath; you are the melody in my heart; you are the very core of all that I am, my cells are you... listen to the birds how they sing; I am weeping right now and I can only imagine what it would be like with you in heaven. I want you so badly, please understand. Who can understand this heart? This heart wants and desires only one thing...no, no, no, no, no, not ministry, no, no, no, no, no, not finances or salvation for the lost...or even feeding children in foreign countries; this heart desires YOU more then anything or any person in my life. YOU, YOU, YOU, YOU!!

✧✧✧

"Who have I in Heaven but thee oh Lord"- David says but true nonetheless with me as well. Must fight!… Fight for what my deepest desire, the calling you have for me in this place, I fight yet am in such grace and peace..

✧✧✧

This love is so deep, how can anyone put words to it, yet these tears in my eyes; the pain of loving you in my heart. You woo me and I am ruined every time. Every time you say come near to me, my bowels are moved, my heart is broken cause I want you so much. You are my romeo... Our love is so deep…

✧✧✧

Look at me my lover, look deep into my heart; I want you so much but can't find you, my everything longs for you. I know what my friend is saying in Song of Solomon when He says He is sick in love.

✧✧✧

You move me to words, you move me to deepness, I got to have more. My soul aches for more; so much that it hurts. This is my song to you, my poetry to you, my life to you. It's the deep calls unto my deep, but it feels like a cave echoing in my heart because I am so hungry and so empty, so lonely for you... my need to is be refilled with you all over again. Day after day coming to that place of falling in love again and be refilled all fresh and new…

✧✧✧

I am so lonely for you my Jesus, so hungry to taste you and see how great and how wonderful you are. You are to me a cold drink after a long run, you are my sun on a cloudy day, you are everything to me, I need you…

✧✧✧

I am so lonely for you; to be with you face to face, to not just have the sensations of your presence knowing you are near, but I want you face to face. To see you, to touch, to hug you! But yet I fear… If I were to have you openly with me and you had to leave I would die of a broken heart… unable to face anything good or bad without you glued by my side. I can't live without you... Jesus!

✦✦✦

✦✦✦

The Bed Chamber

Deep kisses is what I need... Deep kisses is what I long for from my master and my King; Take me away in the bedchamber, take me away to your bedroom, in the purity of your love.. the ecstasy of being with you fully. You take my breath away in your Holiness and in your beauty... purity I say, purity of love with my King. Not as a husband and a wife but something deeper of two souls that collide in the Spiritual realm. Because you are so real.

✧✧✧

Never standing alone in the dark without you beside me; that is how real you are to me. Looking around and seeing no one yet seeing you so clear, our heart beats faster at the sight of each other and then....
Pure eruptions come alive inside...as I have the revelation that YOU want ME.... How can that be? You want me now, I know, it's the look in your eyes, you want me, no it can't be I tell myself but yet it comes out, Jesus... You want me...You need me... the explosions of love and intimacy erupts like never before and our love becomes an affair that everyone talks about... an affair of you wanting me and me wanting you... it's a scandal. It's pure, it's Holy... it's. it's PRAYER!

✧✧✧

I call it my hiding place; I pull up the covers and worship you in the quietness, you need me to be here, you put me here, you put me here. So we can be alone. So we can be ALONE. Because you want me, it's true! I love hiding, you call it the secret place, I call it my hiding place.

✧✧✧

Oh no! I grieve to leave that place... I grieve and beg, please say I can stay... the hours are but minutes with you. And I know your always with me, BUT the secret place is priceless, only few people know that place... like Peter, James, John and I...it's where You Need US….

✧✧✧

How many know? Not many know who you are, You taste me, you taste us together and you wont let me go and I don't want to go... it's different when your in love and you spend time together in the bedchamber... "He's always with you they say" but they do not understand the depths of being alone in the hiding place. <u>Friends don't go to the secret place, only lovers do.</u>

✧✧✧

In this intimate place the touching begins... where you come with your Holy Presence and rub your anointing on me and I rub my fragrance of Worship upon you and we become one because I have the understanding that you love me, want me and need me and that I love you, want you and need you: their is a deep love that explodes, filled with Glory... Hours go by, then I leave only to hurry back because I am addicted to the way your love feels. And you woo me back because your addicted to the way my love feels to you! Your so Holy!

✧✧✧

Believe me when I say he is so beautiful and so full of glory that He makes me so hungry every moment I am alive... it's by His Spirit that I come to know such deep riches in Him.

✧✧✧

I am dreaming of you once again- my heart is moved... I want to be with you so much sometimes it hurts.

(Dearest Reader) The Longing... Can you feel that dear reader?... That longing... here is the definition of longing- to have a strong wish or desire... it's a pulling upward. Amen!

✧✧✧

Jesus, Am I going to lift off the ground? I feel like a magnetic pull taking me to you.

✧✧✧

Oh no, shshsh! Don't tell, but such a jealousy rises within my heart when I see you with other people. Not a bad thing, but a longing to be the best I can be at loving you and being with you and also receiving you! My heart longs to be your prize, longs to be the apple of your eye, I want you to see me, I want to please you, my King.

✧✧✧

Can you see the hidden parts of my heart? Because if you look deeply, inside you will see two things, a heart full of you my love and a heart with a hole in it. A hole because that is the space you leave empty till I see you face to face. It's that hole that keeps me running after you... it's that blessed hole that keeps me hungry and ever seeking your face.

✧✧✧

Jesus, read these words I sing...you are my lover and you matter to me, your more real then the sunshine or the stars at night. You belong to me...

✧✧✧

Let us go into your bedchamber where we can share our love of intimate secrets and desires. Our love will spill over into a deep intense worship without even trying. A holy communion between us. An exchange me giving you myself and you giving me your self. Just like when you took James, Peter and John to the top of the mountain and they were in such ecstasy they could not bear the thought of leaving and wanted to start building homes there. Oh Jesus let us stay in that place together for days and days, if you allowed Moses then so can I. We can take our place in this World with great success if people can take knowledge and note that we have been with you! (Acts 4:13) I love to be under the covers with you and the shades drawn and were snuggled up together. No one knows were together, people get so busy in the World they don't realize what fun it is to be with you! I feel sorry for them, they don't realize your the source of all their needs, they keep looking to someone instead of going to the very source, YOU! But alas!! I know, and I love being with you, your the best kept secret this world has yet to find out!

✧✧✧

✧✧✧

The Hiding Place, Still...

It's called the Hiding Place Still, cause I am still here with you or I have come again to be with you; your all I desire to talk about...

✧✧✧

A place where we run to when we feel so alone and lost, refused and rejected... We come sometimes because someone stole our heart and put it back broken. I love the hiding place, because it's safe... no one can hurt you there, help! Sometimes I get stuck there, again like James, Peter and John... but unlike them they eventually left; tears come down my face and I cannot leave my hiding place. So hungry for more of you unless I perish, yes die. Some may not understand, but I call it a new form of hunger... Oh, Jesus come and touch me lest I die of a broken and empty heart. Look at me do you see me, I need you Jesus, help me I am so weak cause I need your love... Come Holy Spirit and wipe away the tears of rejection, the tears of loneliness, cause of needing you so much...

✧✧✧

My heart longs for that special touch only you can give; in the hiding place no one can find me, they look for me but cannot find me, for I am not; for God has taken me away yet again... deep calls unto deep... Here I am Lord ready to take flight in the big vast depth of who you are; You longing for me and me longing for You..selah

✧✧✧

Can you hear the simple cry, the simple lonely girl longing to never leave the hiding place... never to leave you... because the hiding place is really you! Yes, you are always with me; but in the hiding place you are my only purpose; to seek your face, that succumbs to only being lost for hours... a meeting can wait, hair appointments; who cares, phone calls; just go to voice mail; I am hiding... please understand, I have found my lover in the hiding place and will not leave Him easily... there is such a richness in here to dwell and live in…

✧✧✧

Come away with me again today... "Hide, hide now", I hear Him say. He wants me again and again, we have so much fun together in the Secret Place of His love. I have fallen in love there over and over with someone so beautiful and who shows me different facets of who He really is.

✧✧✧

Simple, sweet, sayings to Him, He loves! And He can never even get enough... Wash over me once again the blood of Jesus and all that I am in you, forever stayed upon this one request, never leave my side, it will never work or never do. You are the answer to my deepest prayer and my deepest dream come true! Carry me away to the skies, lets be together and I will yell to the highest mountain top, all my love and cravings are towards you my sweetie!

✧✧✧

I pray in the Spirit to stir the depths in which I am called, I look deep into the Song of Solomon and desire you more then the readings I read on the page. How can this be, a love so deep with a man I have never even seen. But Jesus!! I have seen you in the windows of my heart and my flesh has experienced you so many times, their is no way to deny how much I love you passionately...

✧✧✧

To look away now I would be a fool, to give up and not pursue you would be the biggest mistake one could ever make... for you have captured my heart, you have ruined me for any other person. You have got to come first or their is no life.

I hear God say~

"Look in the depths of the sea and you will see my love for you so deep; Like birds flying through the air above; my Spirit soars and blesses to a never ending well that springs up, even in the biggest drought you will be satisfied."

You say~

"I want you, but the most amazing this is... you want me dear Lord... I desire true intimacy with you and yet you do so with me... me touching you with my words and expression of worship, you touching me with your presence and very breath of life. This is how a person can never be satisfied.. cause you breath new life... that propels me to seek you more and more."

✧✧✧

It's not made up, it's, you, your, so REAL! You melt my insides; You are the only one that makes my heart sing of true love... Jump, dance, shout, You know my name and You love me, You need me, You use me... is their any greater thing?

✧✧✧

✧✧✧

Seriously considering this phrase…You; the one I desire to worship, to kiss! (the word "worship" in the Strong's Concordance means "to kiss")

✦✦✦

Dreams & Hope Deferred

Oh Lord, I have to ask, Why? Why do you put big dreams inside a person. Impossible dreams that cannot be lived without and left feeling woe and undone. Because what if they do not come to pass. What if it's... it's a dream and that is it.. a dream; No! God, if you put something inside then YOU must make it come to pass. I must not strive for that which is impossible; all you said I had to do was Believe.

✦✦✦

Yes, I will walk through those doors as they open. I will not stall or linger in the door way (pray for hours wondering if it is your will) but will go straight on in as you promised with the vision in my heart... But God... Where is the door? Where is the vision, I have seen for so long? I want it, I crave it with every ounce of who I am; I need it... Dreams Come! Dear Lord, take me on the path of what we have dreamed together since I was eight years old.

✧✧✧

It's as though this dream will quench all the dryness in my parched mouth. It's fruit will be like eating the fatted calf as they did in Biblical times. So hungry for you, so hungry for the dream, for the vision to behold, taste and be...

✧✧✧

Seconds turn into, minutes and minutes turn into hours... hours... days.... days... weeks... months... years... years. How much longer dearest Jesus? Let me be young to enjoy the promise I pray, let me be seasoned and equipped to enjoy the dream and the vision you have given me.

✧✧✧

My teachers have laughed. They have set me aside as waste, do you not see me papa? Where do I fit in? Again searching and wondering. What do I think of myself with such dreams and visions, surely I must be making them up, surely they are all of the flesh Lord. Nobody knows my name, help me Lord. I am sick and want to be found.

✧✧✧

Years go by and still I am this sitting duck, waiting for the flow of the river to rise. Yes, sometimes a small creek, a gusher comes and I flow along a very short distant only to be sitting along the bank side again. I see the other ducks that were with me soar on by... but what happened? Now I am angry, (only cause you said I could be, as long as I sin not) but I am angry as I see they are no longer ducks but swans living their "life", their "dream"... What is wrong with me? Why can't anyone see me? Lord I cry to you but I can't find you; except a still small voice that whispers two words... "Trust Me". So I cry the more, praying, wishing for something, something to happen.

YES!, Then it begins to happen.. people begin to see and take notice! Thank you Jesus, I minister unto you and find great favor among Kings; But, I have a problem, I have been forgotten for so long, like an unwanted dog that wonders the streets for so long! And when that dog is ready to be accepted and celebrated; an awful thing happens Lord... It, I, become grateful. So grateful, so grateful, that I feel foolish and ever so often as someone throws their arms in the air to declare God's goodness over me, I flinched because I think I am about to get hit again like that abused dog that has been hit with rolled up newspaper. That dog that is wondering the streets. But atlas, they don't hit, scold or reprimand... but are taken back and think how strange this girl seems to be... and their thoughts of truth or are they lies I can not tell, but it becomes yelling in my ears. I am so dependent on you Lord!

✦✦✦

✦✦✦

Psalm 25

To You, O Lord, I lift up my soul.

O my God, I trust in You;
Let me not be ashamed;
Let not my enemies triumph over me.

Indeed, let no one who waits on You be ashamed;
Let those be ashamed who deal treacherously without cause.

Show me Your ways, O Lord;
Teach me Your paths.

Lead me in Your truth and teach me,
For You *are* the God of my salvation;
On You I wait all the day.

Remember, O Lord, Your tender mercies and Your lovingkindnesses,
For they *are* from of old.

Do not remember the sins of my youth, nor my transgressions;
According to Your mercy remember me,
For Your goodness' sake, O Lord.

Good and upright *is* the Lord;
Therefore He teaches sinners in the way.

The humble He guides in justice,
And the humble He teaches His way.

All the paths of the Lord *are* mercy and truth,

To such as keep His covenant and His testimonies.

For Your name's sake, O Lord,
Pardon my iniquity, for it *is* great.

Who *is* the man that fears the Lord?
Him shall He[a] teach in the way He[b] chooses.

He himself shall dwell in prosperity,
And his descendants shall inherit the earth.

The secret of the Lord *is* with those who fear Him,
And He will show them His covenant.

My eyes *are* ever toward the Lord,
For He shall pluck my feet out of the net.

Turn Yourself to me, and have mercy on me,
For I *am* desolate and afflicted.

The troubles of my heart have enlarged;
Bring me out of my distresses!

Look on my affliction and my pain,
And forgive all my sins.

Consider my enemies, for they are many;
And they hate me with cruel hatred.

Keep my soul, and deliver me;
Let me not be ashamed, for I put my trust in You.

Let integrity and uprightness preserve me,
For I wait for You.
Redeem Israel, O God,
Out of all their troubles!

Rejection

I trusted this person as you lead me Lord. I poured out my heart, they thought of me as a flake. What do you say of this my Lord? Oh yes, I wear the coat of many colors, yes favor comes only long enough for it to be stripped away yet again...and to start all over... years now turn into decades.... When God when?

✧✧✧

Hurry, I am getting weak, hurry I am having trouble seeing, hurry another wave has crushed me again, hurry the rolled up newspaper doesn't feel like paper any more but cut glass it scrapes across me like a whip. And the whip keeps hitting the same spot crushing down across my side leaving black and blue wounds, my heart needs bandages so the blood wont get on my shirt; so people wont see the wounds so openly.

✧✧✧

Gasp! Their they are again, their with the "friends" holding onto that rolled up newspaper and they have a knife, but what are they doing with a knife? Oh no, help..gulp,. my heart....*Wounded.. it happened so fast, he put the knife in my chest cavity and having trouble breathing now... I am in shock, so hurt that I cannot even cry. This one is gonna take some time....

◇◇◇

Oh no, Help me Lord, am having trouble breathing. My heart aches so much because of the poison of my friends that are now my enemy's. The poison of their lips...their words. I am wounded and crushed again..
Lord hear me, I pray!
Please don't give me more scriptures God, give me my promise! I don't want to cry myself to sleep any more. Don't want to defend or give myself away to people, Cause people always let me down. "Hope thou in God for the help of His countenance" Psalm 42:5
But my God, You, Oh Lord will not let me down. I know this!

◇◇◇

But why Lord, where is your truth; where is your justice!! I shall not be angry or shall I... Another one again slips a knife in my back, they are so smooth and it's so kindly done. Not a stranger but a brother Lord. They did it so clean, nicely, but deeper this time then before.. They did it in love so the wound wont effect them or their ministries. Right? Jesus, does that make it "okay".

✧✧✧

Forgotten! I don't know; misplaced, put on the shelf again. I have had so much favor, so much love, from a real person! I remember the encounter you gave me in that meeting. Lord, an encounter that lasted for three months! I cried myself to sleep cause I was so grateful that you gave such favor to me? Grateful because I now I had a mentor that took me under their wing and love me as a son/daughter to teach things in Ministry and even used me in my calling! So excited, I always call my mentor my "gift" because I met them on that special day!

One Thing.

But all this to remind me of "One Thing"...just one thing, ONE... You my Sweetie. It's a constant reminder that you are my shelter, my Prince, my Mentor, my Knight in shinning amour!

✧✧✧

Prophetic Word of the Lord...

I hear you say, "Lay your head back and think of me and your sorrow shall turn into my delight; The places and things that I have prepared for you is but a moment away. There is a special place you have found through your seeking, through your desire; and like with Mary it shall not be taken away from you, Seek Now"... I hear Him say "Seek now and I shall surely show you a better way than those before you or their ways they have gone to get ahead. Oh Listen to me my sweet, sweet beloved ones, their is a place beside me as in the days of Noah, still their is a place I have open for you. Do what ever you have to do, come... run, walk, crawl, but come in that place of the cleft of the rock; and I will not leave you dry. The hardest part for you is getting there, not getting there like you suppose; but it's opening up the time to come. For time is the biggest thing that will stop you, it is the biggest enemy among the Church, among people that love me. If only they would take the time and lean their head upon my chest like John my disciple did, they are so many benefits and rewards that come from that place beside me. Listen now and hear the birds... listen how they sing my praise all day... be like the birds children! Carefree and happy; listen to the song they sing; for they only sing what they have heard sung. If you abide with me, I will give you a new song this day and it will be a song for keeps. A song you will always remember; cause you did not hear it mans way but you heard it; in the Spirit, in the Secret place, in the cleft of the rock.

Behold the days, they are long and times goes by, but look now at your day today for this is the outcome of your tomorrow. You are sowing what you do today for your outcome tomorrow. So take hold of today, let go of yesterdays, let go of opinions, let go of your surroundings and grab hold of me and don't let go of what is most important, For I am the Lord God and I hold all of your promises; I hold all of your dreams; I hold all of your visions, all your tomorrows. Come to me and I will make the impossible possible.. Come to me till I make all your enemies a footstool. Break not away but stay, stay, stay, stay in the Secret place and let me take care of everything,; let me take care of you!." -Saith the Lord.

✧✧✧

You are so beautiful and so sweet, Lord Jesus I need you and I come. I desire to come to that place where you will take care of me. Where you will make my dreams come true, because after all they are your dreams to start with…

✧✧✧

✧✧✧

Ministry Aches

Ministry of Brokenness

How is it so, such a passion comes to minister and to be used by you my God. I hunger and desire to minister your word, I cry as I go to bed cause of the passion and longing within to get out what you have put deep inside... But then, what is this? I get into the office of ministering and as I minister, the longing to go off and be alone with you beckons me, as I minister you come with such a power; I stand back and watch you move and speak... but deep inside I just want to run away and hide back in that secret place. I am so comfortable in that place when it's just me and you. Remember Lord? I was social, remember Lord I had tons of friends... now what gives me the greatest joy is being alone... alone with you. I long for it, crave it and not only that... this place I have come to with you, is a place I need it to survive. I would not be able to live or breathe but would literally die. My only source of life and joy comes from being with you, for YOU are my life!! YOU are my breath Sweetie and no one can take you away from me! YOU wont let them for I belong to you! And because of my love for you... you give me so much love for my family and friends and for strangers... God you are amazing!

✧✧✧

Storms, Hurts & Seasons!

You did it once again. I couldn't even write because of the "trying of my faith being much more precious then gold or silver that perishes." Was such a hard season my Love, how did you sustain me to get through it? How did I keep going? All because of You that is how.. you are the love of my life. I have a sweeter love for you now more then ever. And that is just how to explain it "Sweeter" maybe I should change your name to Sweetie huh?

✧✧✧

Oh Jesus.. that season was so hard. I wanted to quit and I wanted to run and I wanted to hide. To hide in a cave, even considered going in to join the monk's for a week or so just to escape! Wanted to cancel meetings for the month. But God, you are my healer! You did it, I went to bed with sores all over my heart and awoke to my wounds all healed up; not even bandaged but they were completely gone! Wow!! You did it, without my even asking God you did it...!! Once again... you are my hero! My rescuer! You are such a wonder, you bring me through the biggest trials as only you can do! You, Jesus you amaze me!

✧✧✧

Ouch My Brother

All sins have been forgotten, my life is hid in Christ, (in you)! No one can see me even if they try, I cannot be found... Just like my brother Enoch, I have a testimony that I please you! But, why does my brother take things you have given me?... For he is like a snake... comes slithering in the grass.. not a stranger, not someone in the World, but my brother sitting beside me worshipping! Dear Jesus, how can that be? It hurt's God. Their tongues are so smooth, yes they are sweet as sugar, because they want something. Wow, so sweet. Then they take and take and then they are gone! And I am left abandon and all alone, I have been robbed and misled and no one knows. They did it so sweetly and politely. My heart aches and only you can take hold of me and bring healing to my sores! Dearest Jesus, I hurt, come and kiss my boo boo and take all the pain away! Let us run free together in a place of freedom right now in this World... no worries but carefree. So in love with you Jesus, you never let me down!

✧✧✧

Lead me dear Lord, so I will not get off the path you have for me. Lead me Papa so I am not wandering about with no vision and for the enemy to trample upon. But atlas, I hear the still small voice and you guide me which way to go.. I hear you call to your bride whom you love. My heart responds with a flutter of excitement as I go along the path you have laid before me! You feed me with meat and my belly is fat because you have filled me with your goodness! O taste and see that the Lord is good! You are exciting Lord! You take my breath away.. You are my hero once again! Let us run together to the fountain of our youth... because you renew my youth like the eagles... You have made me forget the ills of a life that was forsaken by the snake in the grass. You have fed me new manna, you have restored my joy once again and now I can sing a new song of love for you my King.

✧✧✧

✧✧✧

Heart Songs

A song of the heart of a people unabridged and sold out to the most loveliest lover known to mankind. Not in a romantic way as lovers in man and woman.. but lovers between God and man... pure ecstasy.

✧✧✧

All I want from you every moment of every day is to kiss you and for you to kiss me over and over again. Tell me again how much you love me, tell me how much you take care of me. I fall in love with you all over again; every day as I see your faithfulness . You constantly are showing me new things about yourself, you amaze me!

✧✧✧

Their is something about you that everywhere I go I know when your in the room. Your presence and all that you are is like a fragrance there... you are so beautiful Jesus... I see you everywhere, I really do! My favorite place to see you is in the eyes of other people. To see you in them full of love and great compassion is completely amazing! It brings tears to my eyes. To see people dancing and frolicking in total abandonment in their love for you, oh Papa it blesses me. It's no wonder people give their all to you, your so tremendously wonderful! You make people happy.

◇◇◇

All I want to do is run away with you... come lets go, where you can be mine and I can be yours on and on loving each other. But wait!! I can hardly catch my breath! Where do you want to go? Lets go to the park again and swing on the swings. Remember how we laughed so hard that we fell down together? We laughed and laughed and rolled down the hill!! Come lets run away together; where no one can find us cause I will be hidden inside you. Yes, hide me, I desire my whole life to be hidden in Christ, what a treasure I am to you my beloved!! YOU ARE MINE! I will share you with no one~yet I will share you with the World!

◇◇◇

You have made me glad and so happy, for your love is better then wine! There is no earthly wine or drug that could make me this happy; your love outshines everything! You take my breath away. And Sweetie, I trust you with my everything because you are the glue that holds everything together! You mean so much to me dear Lord. No one can hurt me, if I take hold of all your promises and forget not to go into the Secret Place...

Where can I go but into that secret place with you, it is the only place I want to stay and dwell. Your love is like no other. You love completes me Lord. There is nothing greater then to secure your love and affection. You bring joy to my heart and all I can do is boast of all your goodness.

✧✧✧

How can one go on like this.... It's supernatural... it's a never ending well that does not run dry. You have captured me to the extreme, I love you... let me say it again and again, I love you!! My passion is for you, your all I think about, your all I desire, all I want. You make me so happy! You are my gift... you and nothing else... you are the love of my life, my passion, my dream, my everything, is YOU!

✧✧✧

I run after you with all my might. I shall find you again. I shall search for you with all my heart and find you and be in your presence yet again. Nothing else can fill me, nothing else will do. I want your fellowship more then anyone else. I love being with you. Because I love you your love spills over to all my family and friends, I love people.. So yes, I run away and hide with you again today. I hide like Moses did on the mountain and come out of that Secret Place full of you and full of your words for myself and for the people around me.

✦✦✦

Your love is so much better then anything this life has to offer. Your love is better then life. Your love is better then what the imagination could ever behold. I imitate you, I am like you and no other... I follow after you and you fill me so their can be no mistake in me. Your blood keeps me and sets me free from all sin and evil.

✦✦✦

Your love is like a fragrance. You fill the room with the very essence of who you are and all "smell" or sense that you are there. All our ruined by one glance of your eyes. We are smitten by the arrangement of your love so beautifully displayed for all to see. How can one even dare to wonder, "How this can be so?" Because of your beauty everyone sees, you are truly a rarity, a King that is so full of pleasures and goodness that it's so hard for the natural man to understand, but something deep inside the loins their is a breath of freshness of soul that comes. A denying of oneself that can't be helped because how can it be? A love so true and pure has stepped deep inside me. All because His fragrance filled the room. And now pure ecstasy and all I can do now is weep if you were ever to leave.

✧✧✧

Crazy in love with this King! You are my everything, the lifter of my head, my knight in shinning amour! My love for you grows like a rare flower that is not allowed to be picked. My love for you grows and grows everyday as I discover new lessons of your love for me and for others! You simply amaze me precious Lord.

✧✧✧

How can it be? What is this? You are like a magnet and all I want to do is be with you... I feel your pull... and I know Lord you feel my pull too. You love to be with me and I cannot get enough of you, so tender, so sweet, so faithful, so beautiful, so grateful to have you in my life. The way you love me makes me so happy and my life is complete. My life is complete as long as I have you near me. Sometimes, like right now in this busy place (airport or where-ever you are) my eyes fill up with tears... I love you so much, you are my everything!

✧✧✧

✧✧✧

Tender moments with you increase day after day.

✧✧✧

Am I okay? I am so in love but how can this be, a person whom I have never seen but have certainly felt many times. You have ruined me, I am no good for anything this World has to offer. You have every part of me and yet I long to have more. I long for more, yet I am full of you. I am full because I am is consumed by you! My thoughts, my actions, my days, my nights, my all in all is filled with you my Sweetie. Their are no mistakes in the way I feel about you; our love is perfect!

✧✧✧

Deep, deep, deep I don't even have to think; cause I feel you take over my thinking. My thoughts are all consumed with you no matter what I do, your there and that is the way I want it. I can't live without you. I can't breath without you. We have the biggest kept secret in the whole World, it's our love for each other. I have no taste for anything but you. You awaken me deep and then deep again.. I am yours completely. I am so in love with you and you are so in love with me. You can't get enough of me, you woo me to yourself and you will not share me with no one! How special I am to you! God....

(pause for a deep moment) I pray for people; that they would love you more and more Everyday!

✧✧✧

Being ugly is a beautiful thing in the sight of God. Treasures untold as one looks and sees himself as he truly is with Christ. Then realizing and coming out of the ugly to be seeing and embracing the beauty you now possess are because of Him.

✧✧✧

Who knows the depth of God? Who can understand this life I have in you; help me someone please; I am aching, longing and wanting more, yet so full and yet so complete in you! Who can understand this wonderful mystery?

✧✧✧

Unbelievable joy erupts inside as I explore your word. It never ceases to grow more and more in understanding. Gently, sweetly you guide me through each loving phrase. Your word truly is like honey to my mouth, a soothing lotion to any cuts I have. You are miraculous and your words are alive. Your words amaze me.

✧✧✧

Refined and polish I stand, not to boast in pride but because of your love and patience I am who you have created. Breathing and living in your sudden vast of life, my eyes are on you and I certainly cannot be denied. You satisfy every longing, every desire, in one instant of your presence... It's you I desire, you I cherish…

✧✧✧

Fill me to overflowing so that my fingers touch the sky and I can taste of your sweetness and gain your revelation love in every part of my being. I want to be in your presence... come Lord, come softly, come sweetly. My life is in need of another touch from you.

✧✧✧

My soul mourns over love for you.. Mourns cause I am so lonely that I need to have you closer here with me now. This longing and sadness is only something you can fill. It's a secret no one knows about. You are my secret, my desire, I long for you in ways that are not humanly possible. I miss you, I need you my lover, my friend.

✦✧✦

✧✦✧

It's the depth that I feel the most... the depth of Heaven that I long for, that's the part I need your touch. Please understand Jesus it's a need... not a want. Satisfy the need and hunger that follows so hard after you. My lips, my tongue need to taste and see that you are good.

✧✧✧

When oh God, when will the longing, yearning in my heart come to rest. Do you feel that inside.. is that how you feel as well? Is it possible that you need me as much as I need you. No! What did I just hear? It cannot be, you said " I need you more..." Oh my God.. how you must ache for me and for all living peoples. If only they knew.

✧✧✧

YOU! You are my God and I will not let go of you. Like men of old testament tenacity. I seek you and I will not let you out of my sight.

✧✧✧

Imagine me papa, in the days when you walked the ancient roads... I would be so embarrassing.. screaming, pleading and never letting you away from my side. They would want to lock me up but you would just say 'let her alone' and I would have my way of loving you every moment here and through out eternity.

✧✧✧

Eternity... I love that word, when I think of you!

✧✧✧

Breaking into my silent World are thoughts of you that beat inside my chest. I love you, I love you.. you are truly altogether lovely. Mere words cannot even understand how wonderful; how sweet; how special you are…

✧✧✧

You are so sweet! So amazing, so real, so familiar! You are my lover, my friend. If you would let me tell you all the ways in which I love you, my hair would turn grey and I would close my eyes for eternity and awake to see you and even still my lips would be expressing my love for you my Sweet Prince!

How vast is your word. It truly amazes me... one look at who I am in that mirror and I glean more and more understanding at who you want me to become or who I am. Your word gives me so much peace, so much understanding. You are the word alive inside me. Your word gives me strength and it keeps me alive. It keeps me full of joy, full of promises that are true and coming to pass. Your word is something I hope in, it brings new life. So simple, so deep, your words penetrate; Holy Spirit you make the word of God so real!

✧✧✧

Minding my own business then suddenly your there, standing before me smiling. Loving me with your eyes, hugging me with your arms. Nothing can take you away from me sweetie, I am yours: You come so quickly that I am overwhelmed, I can't help it and cry, your love is so amazing. You show up and it melts me to an overwhelming love that cannot be expressed. I am undone again, weeping softly...so thankful yet so desperate for you to not leave. Such agony to have your presence lift in any way, so frustrating that after awhile my flesh tries to fight sitting still... "no, no, no," flesh I say. Sweetie, please stay and don't go my love, not yet.. not yet and of course you stay.

✧✧✧

Gushers of longings shoot through me as I need you more and more. So hungry, so in need of another touch from you...

✦✦✦

I love you, it's all I can say at times. Nothing else comes to my heart and mind...I love you... I am a life that is totally surrendered to you and no other. I love you, you amaze me, your wooing me again and sometimes it's more then I can take.

✦✦✦

Your loving me, I feel it... your wanting me and me wanting you! It's wonderful, yes we have a groovy love that is so unbelievable! Kiss me again my Sweetie..

✦✦✦

Last night was so amazing, so full of hurt. How can I explain it to people Lord. The love we have together hurts, especially at night. Not a physical pain kind of hurt, but a holy emotional hurt. You break my heart nearly every night. I love you. The words used to mean so much but my love for you is so deep that now their are no words that can convey the vastness of how I feel about you. Like Solomon said "I am sick in love". It must be a Supernatural love, a Supernatural longing... You make hunger so beautiful...

✦✦✦

Nothing left to say... nothing left to do... just one thing though, to love you more and more and more for now and for all eternity..

✦✦✦

Everything is so beautiful. You, you make everything so beautiful. You make people so beautiful. I am amazed by the way you love people. The way you touch them with yourself as they offer up just a teeny portion of themselves, you take it and fill it!

✦✦✦

Your ways are so high it is too hard to understand. Holy Spirit help me to comprehend this great plan you have created. This dream you have placed inside will never come to pass unless you bring it about.

✦✦✦

I am in love with you and your in love with me that is all I need to know. Come and sit by my side and together we will discover what it is like to be in love all over again. You are my best friend, come and breath fresh revelation in my Spirit, into my knowing. Wisdom belongs to you but yet to me too because I know and am involved and intertwined with you.

✧✧✧

Yes! I am involved with someone. I am intertwined and one with someone I can not even see. But so real and so wonderful it goes beyond imagination and beyond any words could ever say.

✧✧✧

Forever and always I shall stand. Though sometimes it feels as though I may slip into the cracks of doubt and unbelief, but your word is like an anchor to my heart and soul.

✧✧✧

CONTINUING ON...

Dear Friend,

May you feel the love of the Father, may you be blessed and highly favored of the Lord! Praying you have felt Him close as you read this simple, yet deep devotionals. Praying you felt Him pull you close and that your relationship is being refreshed and renewed!

I encourage you to go through this book as many times as you need! Underline, high light, make these words your words!! Journal on the open pages (or anywhere) your own Songs of Desire. Let this book bring a passion to capture your heart in a pure romance that only He can give you! A Supernatural love that's so amazing!

Keep Going!!

Love you and Praying for You!!

✧✧✧

✧✧✧

Made in the USA
Columbia, SC
05 May 2018